DARWIN & EVOLUTION
The Big Idea

Paul Strathern was born in London and studied philosophy at Trinity College, Dublin. He was a lecturer at Kingston University where he taught philosophy and mathematics. He is a Somerset Maugham prize-winning novelist. He is also the author of the *Philosophers in 90 Minutes* series. He wrote *Mendeleyev's Dream* which was shortlisted for the Aventis Science Book Prize, *Dr. Strangelove's Game: A History of Economic Genius*, *The Medici: Godfathers of the Renaissance*, *Napoleon in Egypt* and most recently, *The Artist, The Philosopher and The Warrior*, which details the convergence of three of Renaissance Italy's most brilliant minds: Leonardo Da Vinci, Niccolo Machiavelli and Cesare Borgia. He lives in London and has three grandchildren.

D1392203

In THE BIG IDEA series:

DARWIN & EVOLUTION
The Big Idea

PAUL STRATHERN

arrow books

Reissued by Arrow Books 2009

3 5 7 9 10 8 6 4

Copyright © Paul Strathern, 1998

Paul Strathern has asserted his right under the Copyright, Designs and
Patents Act, 1988, to be identified as the author of this work.

This book is sold subject to the condition that it shall not, by way
of trade or otherwise, be lent, resold, hired out, or otherwise
circulated without the publisher's prior consent in any form of
binding or cover other than that in which it is published and
without a similar condition including this condition being
imposed on the subsequent purchaser.

First published in Great Britain in 1998 by Arrow Books

The Random House Group Limited
20 Vauxhall Bridge Road, London SW1V 2SA

www.rbooks.co.uk

Addresses for companies within The Random House Group Limited
can be found at: www.randomhouse.co.uk/offices.htm

The Random House Group Limited Reg. No. 954009

A CIP catalogue record for this book
is available from the British Library

ISBN 9780099238225

The Random House Group Limited supports The Forest Stewardship
Council (FSC), the leading international forest certification organisation.
All our titles that are printed on Greenpeace approved FSC certified paper
carry the FSC logo. Our paper procurement policy can be found at
www.rbooks.co.uk/environment.

Mixed Sources
Product group from well-managed
forests and other controlled sources
www.fsc.org Cert no. TT-COC-2139
© 1996 Forest Stewardship Council

FSC

Typeset in Bembo by SX Composing DTP, Rayleigh, Essex
Printed and bound in the United Kingdom by
CPI Cox & Wyman, Reading, RG1 8EX

CONTENTS

INTRODUCTION

The idea of evolution now seems so evident to us that it's difficult to imagine how the world appeared without it. Darwin has suffered the same fate as Freud, who said: 'I hope one day they ask: what was so special about that chap Freud? Everything he said was perfectly obvious.' On the other hand (again like Freud), when Darwin's ideas are fully examined they can appear to be completely unscientific, or even meaningless. In the final analysis 'Survival of the fittest' really means nothing more than 'Survival of what survives'.

Yet either way, Darwin is undeniably one of the few thinkers who has changed our entire notion of how we see ourselves and the world around us. After him, things would never be the same. And there was no going back. After Darwin, man ceased for ever to be a privileged species.

Darwin came at the end of the revolution which started in the 16th century with Copernicus. The earth orbited the sun: we were no longer the centre of the universe. Even more significantly, it was found that scientific laws held true in the heavens. (Previously, these had been thought to apply only on earth.) Darwin completed this revolution by showing how science even applied to life itself. Everything was scientific, and humanity was no longer the centre of anything – just another species in an evolving scientific process. At first this was unacceptable and shocking. It undermined our very idea of what we were. But human beings are resilient creatures. The genetic factors which produced them have not endured five billion years of evolution for nothing. Contrary to prediction, such self-understanding has not reduced us to 'scientific automata'. Like the man who put us in this predicament, we remain 'human, all too human'.

SURVIVAL OF THE UNFIT

Charles Robert Darwin was born on February 12th 1809. His family tree contains an unusual concentration of distinguished figures. These include the famous pottery designer and manufacturer Josiah Wedgwood, and Francis Galton the physicist and founder of eugenics (the scientific study of hereditary improvement of the human race, which was later discredited by events in the 20th century).

But most interesting of all was Charles Darwin's grandfather, Erasmus Darwin, a man of boundless intellectual energy and some originality. Along with Wedgwood, James Watt the inventor of the steam engine, and Benjamin Franklin the American statesman and inventor, Erasmus Darwin formed the Lunar Society, the Birmingham-based scientific club which was regarded as second only to the Royal Society (despite the inevitable collective name for its members). Arguably, it was Erasmus Darwin who came up with the first serious explanation of evolution – though he failed to think this idea through in any depth. This was partly because the medium he chose to publicize his ideas was not conducive to deep cerebral analysis. Erasmus Darwin was one of the few serious scientists since Lucretius (*fl* first century BC) who opted to promulgate his ideas in the form of epic poetry. (Indeed, George III almost made him poet laureate, until it was discovered that he believed in the abolition of royalty.)

With so much originality in the family background, an exception was bound to appear sooner or later. This came in the form of Robert Darwin, Charles's father – a man who aspired to mediocrity, and was to make this his life's achievement. No mean feat, judging from his appearance: Robert Darwin was 6ft 2ins tall, and weighed 24 stone (before he gave up consulting the scales in disgust). A domineering man, by turns irascible and affable, he inherited money and became a doctor. The medical speciality he chose to pursue was rich patients, and he became famous throughout Shropshire for his bedside manner. (Only when large fees were in the offing did he actually listen to anyone.) The generous gratitude of rich women suffering from 'ailments' in this pre-psychological era was sufficient to make him a very rich man, and Robert Darwin took his place amongst the emerging well-off professional class.

The social niceties (or boredom) of Jane Austen were now giving way to the more stifling era of Victorian respectability. Yet despite its risible qualities, such smug orthodoxy was hard-won — both in general, and in the Darwinian particular. Social conditions were turbulent in early 19th century England: this was the period of the Peterloo Massacre and the Tolpuddle Martyrs. Also, there appears to have been a streak of latent mental instability in the Darwins: Erasmus was 'volatile', and Robert's brother (Charles's uncle) committed suicide.

Young Charles did his best to emulate his father, and was soon a budding mediocrity. He even kept a solemn diary. (Despite worldwide adventure and earth-shattering ideas, Darwin's autobiographical style was to be pure *Diary of a Nobody* from the word go.) Charles was largely looked after by his doting older sisters until the age of eight, when his mother died. From then on he was totally looked after by his doting older sisters – who provided him with warm rugs and soothing warm drinks, constant mollycoddling sufficient to induce a lifetime of hypochondria, and their idea of an education. The Darwins, the Wedgwoods and the Galtons were something of an extended family, and female cousins and aunts all took turns looking after this human doll.

Charles Darwin was eventually dislodged from the centre of the universe and sent to Shrewsbury, the local Victorian public school. This provided a sort of negative image of the education provided by doting sentimental Victorian maidens. Nothing was taught but the classics, and the regularly caned pupils consisted mostly of unruly squires' sons who terrorized nearby farms kidnapping pigs, milkmaids and the like.

The bewildered Darwin began taking an interest in nature, collecting specimens, and conducting his own chemistry experiments – during the quieter periods when his fellow pupils were out vandalizing the neighbourhood. The headmaster was outraged, and upbraided Darwin in front of the entire school for 'wasting his time'. As Darwin succinctly put it: 'The school as a means of education to me was simply a blank.'

But Darwin wasn't quite such a little wimp as he'd have us believe. Away from his sisters, he soon became interested in sport – which in those days involved brutality towards animals, rather than fellow participants. Father was furious: 'You care for nothing but shooting, dogs, and rat-catching, and you will be a disgrace to yourself and all your family.' The last was too awful to contemplate, and at the age of 16 young Charles was hoicked out of school and sent to Edinburgh University to study medicine, just as his father had before him.

In those days Edinburgh University had one of the finest medical schools in Europe. Previously, the best students had travelled to Leiden and Utrecht, but this practice had ceased with the Napoleonic Wars. Yet even the top medical schools were still gruesome spots, firmly grounded in the sawbones era. The sensitive young Darwin was horrified when he had to attend operations, where surgery was carried out with no anaesthetic and buckets of blood beneath the table. ('Rum to put him out, steadfast assistants to hold him down, and a stout heart' were reckoned to be a surgeon's best aids.)

Once again Darwin found himself drawn towards the byways of biology. He joined the Plinian Natural History Society, and here he formed a friendship with the zoologist Dr Robert Grant, who also lectured in anatomy.

Both were obsessed with collecting specimens, and Grant took Darwin along on his expeditions. Together they regularly combed the Firth of Forth foreshore at low tide, collecting marine life and plants. These they would then examine under a microscope, and dissect. Any original finds would be sorted, according to the classification which had been proposed by the great Swedish botantist Linnaeus just 70 years previously.

Linnaeus had opened up the entire field of biology with his revolutionary system of classification. Initially, this divided plants into classes and groups, giving each a latin generic name and a descriptive adjective. For example *Rosa damascena* for the scented velvety pink damask rose – which had acquired different local names in the various regions where it grew throughout the world. Later Linnaeus extended this form of classification to insects and all forms of animal eg, *Homo sapiens*, the so-called wise hominid. He even extended this latin nomenclature to his own professional name – adopting the pseudonym Linnaeus, after a linden tree (Swedish: 'Linnaea') in his garden. It is easy for us to see how Linnaeus's system set the scene for the idea of evolution; though Linnaeus himself strongly objected to such talk. Having just classifed all the species as different, he was unlikely to welcome the idea that they were really all the same, in the beginning. In Linnaeus's view the species were immutable, and had been since the Creation – with no new species appearing, and none becoming extinct.

Darwin's new-found friend and mentor Dr Grant disagreed with Linnaeus on this last point. Grant was all in favour of the ideas put forward by the 83-year-old Jean Lamarck, the greatest living French biologist. Born into an impoverished aristocratic family, Lamarck had risen to become royal botanist to Louis XVI. During the French Revolution the King and anyone remotely to do with him – such as royal botanists and aristocrats without sufficient cash to bribe their way out of the country – were guillotined wholesale throughout the land. But Lamarck somehow survived all this, to emerge as a professor of zoology in revolutionary Paris. This miraculous feat of evolution may well have coloured his scientific ideas.

Lamarck put forward an early form of evolution. (Indeed, the statue of Lamarck in the Luxembourg Gardens in Paris chauvinistically claims him as 'the founder of evolution'.) Independently of Darwin's grandfather Erasmus, and some years later than him, Lamarck came up with the idea that species of animals and plants were not fixed, they evolved. Unlike Erasmus Darwin, Lamarck chose to back up his idea with something more convincing than poetic inspiration. Lamarck pursued the implications of his idea, analyzing it – though alas his results were almost equally poetic. In his view, the formative feature in evolution was environment. As, for example, in the cat family. The difference between the spitting mountain wildcat and the purring domestic pussycat was purely due to their different environments. Nature could induce all kinds of changes in animals. For instance, the giraffe had a long neck because for generations it had been reaching for high leaves. This led Lamarck to the view that 'acquired characteristics are inherited' ie, abilities developed by one generation could be passed on to the next. This sounds plausible enough, especially when one considers such families as the Bachs or the Borgias. But the idea doesn't stand up to closer examination. Roderigo Borgia (Pope Alexander VI) did not pass on his ruthless political skills to his children Cesare and Lucrezia. What they inherited was a familial propensity to viciousness and amorality, which they used to develop their *own* political skills. These had to be learned, they were not inherited.

Most Lamarckians like Dr Grant believed in this notion of 'inherited characteristics'. However, Lamarck's views on evolution were shunned by orthodox biologists on religious grounds (they contradicted the Bible's view of a simultaneous fixed creation). Listening to discussions of such ideas between Dr Grant and fellow members of the Plinian Natural History Society, Darwin found his interest awakened in the early history of the Earth. How had it all begun? Was it possible that this too had evolved? What exactly was life?

Only rarely has it been possible for us to ask such questions about life and the universe *and follow them with meaningful original speculation.* Such moments have frequently heralded profound shifts in human knowledge. Thales began ancient Greek philosophy with such speculation; following the Renaissance, Descartes and Galileo helped revive philosophy and science with similar questions. Darwin now began asking such questions – but like the rest of us, he could come up with nothing resembling a meaningful original answer. The time was not yet ripe: his intellectual equipment was pitifully wanting, and he knew almost nothing of the subjects concerned – yet he couldn't help speculating nonetheless. (We all know the feeling.)

No one was particularly impressed by earnest bumbling young Darwin. Dr Grant and his fellow natural history buffs patronized him in friendly fashion — but Father was less tolerant. Darwin had spent two years at Edinburgh supposedly studying medicine, yet what did he have to show for it? All he seemed to be interested in was such things as the sexual organs of plants, the proportions of female sea slugs and the liquid intake of the bladderwort. Only with regard to the human body were medical students expected to take an interest in such subjects — either academically or socially. There was obviously something wrong with the boy. In 1837 Darwin was hoicked out of Edinburgh and sent to Cambridge, to study divinity. The only thing to do was get him into the church.

Enrolled as a divinity student at Christ's College, Darwin duly conformed to the role expected of a typical future clergyman. He lived a hectic social life at parties and dinner clubs, ran up large wine bills, and returned to his former sporting pastimes, attending a succession of fox hunts, pigeon shoots, and days out fishing on the river. But maiming, killing and eating the very nature which had previously provided him with specimens wasn't quite the same thing. His heart just wasn't in it.

Fortunately Darwin soon got to hear about the weekly open house held by the Reverend John Henslow, the professor of botany. These soirées attracted a characteristically Victorian company: avid naturalists eager to encounter fellow enthusiasts, earnest young ordinands driven to extra-curricular interests by the tedium of their rigidly classical and theological studies, serious-minded dons interested in the company of serious-minded young men, and so forth.

The Rev Professor Henslow was 32 years old, but had much in common with Darwin. He too had rich parents, who had despatched him to Cambridge to study for the church, where he had discovered that his real interest lay in science. By 26, Henslow had become professor of minerology and curate of St Mary's, close to the Botanical Gardens. The latter was where his real interest lay, and together with volunteers from his soirées he set about a scientific restoration of the gardens to their former glory. (Many examples of the unique flora discovered in Australia had first been transplanted here.)

In those days botany was regarded at Cambridge much as structuralism is today – a useful hobby for undergraduates, diverting their energies from uprooting and deconstructing things of genuine value. The previous professor of botany had held the post for 63 years, had decided against giving lectures during the last 30 years of his tenure, and was eventually discovered to have left Cambridge altogether some years ago. When Henslow succeeded to the chair, he immediately set about reviving the subject. He instituted a new course of botany lectures which began attracting scores of undergraduates, and was soon leading regular weekend expeditions into the nearby fens in search of rare wetland species. Henslow had by now acquired a reputation for scientific knowledge in a variety of other fields – ranging through physics, chemistry and geology. His botany lectures contained far-reaching references, appearing to link the Earth and its sciences in one unfolding enterprise.

Darwin was fascinated, by both the man and his knowledge. Within weeks he was hanging on Henslow's every word. Henslow evidently appreciated such dogged appreciation, and Darwin soon accompanied him everywhere. Things eventually reached the point where

Darwin acquired the nickname 'the man who walks with Henslow'. Uncannily echoing Dr Grant, Henslow was precisely 13 years older than Darwin. Darwin had found himself a new father figure.

In 1830 Darwin eventually began applying himself to the subjects he should have been studying, and graduated the next year with a mediocre degree. He was not looking forward to life as a country parson, and his early propensity to hypochondria took a turn for the worse.

Around this time, Henslow was offered the post of unpaid naturalist aboard HMS *Beagle*, which was due to set sail for South America on a surveying trip for the Admiralty. Henslow didn't want to leave Cambridge, so he offered the job to Darwin – who leapt at the chance. Unfortunately Father decided this was no post for a future clergyman, and refused his permission. But Charles was still something of a family favourite, especially amongst the daughters, female cousins and aunts. Old sourpuss was eventually prevailed upon to allow his son's wish. Just this once.

The surveying trip planned for HMS *Beagle*

was set to include the east and west coasts of South America, a large number of Pacific islands, Australia and a circumnavigation of the globe. It was expected to take around two years. (Such 'estimates' were pure fantasy, these trips often taking two or three times their allotted span.)

When one considers the projected trip, the *Beagle* was astonishingly small. A refitted three-masted bark, it was just 90 feet long (a few paces longer than a cricket pitch), with its main deck only 4 feet above the water level. Its captain was an intelligent 26-year-old Old Harrovian called Robert FitzRoy, grandson of the 18th century prime minister Lord Grafton. FitzRoy had taken over when the previous captain had committed suicide in mid-voyage. The crew of 74 men and youths were almost all younger than their captain. Though few of them would have looked it: the hard life below decks in the Royal Navy soon withered the bloom of youth.

It was customary to take a botanist on such surveying trips. (On his voyage to explore Australia just 70 years previously, Captain Cook had taken one of Linnaeus's pupils.) But FitzRoy wasn't interested in taking just *any* botanist.

During the previous trip he had been forced to endure, at close quarters and for months on end, an enthusiastic bore of the first water. (One can't help wondering whether this had played a part in the captain's suicide.) Fortunately FitzRoy liked Darwin from the word go. Darwin was different: here was a botanist he could speak to, and share ideas with. Darwin was indeed a different type of botanist: one who had no qualifications what-soever, and whose practical experience was limited to amateur weekend rambles through the countryside. (Even the ship's doctor was required to have a carpenter's certificate.)

Darwin also took to FitzRoy, who believed in keeping his ship well-equipped with things that mattered on a long voyage. The ship's library contained over 250 books, including all volumes of the latest *Encyclopedia Britannica* (then, as now, a must for settling bets). These books occupied nearly 50 feet of shelf space – not bad in a ship 90 feet long, nine tenths of whose crew were illiterate. Darwin had no idea what he was doing, or what he was letting himself in for. But he was all enthusiasm for the coming adventure.

'The Owl and the Pussycat went to sea
In a beautiful pea-green boat.
They took some honey, and plenty of money,
Wrapped up in a five pound note.'

Darwin confided that this trip would be his 'second birth'. And he was right. During the course of this long voyage the rather odd biological specimen, a caterpillar of sorts, was to become transformed into a scientific butteryfly of truly astonishing refinement and proportions.

The transformation started quickly. Henslow had seen the voyage as Darwin's big opportunity to extend his scientific range. To encourage this, he had given Darwin the first volume of Charles Lyell's *Principles of Geology* – with the cryptic instruction that he should read it, but refrain from believing in it. Darwin was soon enthusiastically devouring this fascinating new work on a subject which he knew almost nothing about. Geology was still an emerging science, its gaps in knowledge filled largely by imaginative speculation. According to orthodox geological thinking of the period, the geographical features of the Earth had been formed by sudden tumultuous upheavals of great magnitude. Entire mountain ranges had been thrust into the sky, and on occasion the whole surface of the Earth had become submerged in flood. This theory was known as Catastrophism, and was in line with the teachings of the Bible – an important requirement for the science of the time.

Lyell disagreed with this theory. According to him the earth's geographical features had been formed by a long and gradual process. Violent upheavals, such as eruptions and earthquakes, certainly played their part, but they only changed the picture in stages. Major geographical features didn't appear all at once: they took time and were subject to the lengthy processes of erosion and deposition. Catastrophes as well as long-term local effects were all cumulative. The Earth's surface had been shaped over a very long period. Such were the controversial new ideas which Darwin was urged not to believe.

The *Beagle* had set sail from Plymouth on 27th December 1831. Darwin was grotesquely seasick and mostly remained in his bunk for the first few days. As the *Beagle* bounced its way across the Bay of Biscay, and his stomach swilled with the swell of the surging sea, the groggy green-faced landlubber applied himself to the more solid upheavals of geology.

In just under three weeks the *Beagle* arrived at São Tiago in the Cape Verde Islands. Miraculously recovered, Darwin rushed ashore to explore. Entering an inland valley he encountered his first tropical vegetation, and was ecstatic with delight. In no time the dense green jungle was denuded as the ship's botanist avidly began collecting specimens.

São Tiago (St Jago) was an ancient volcano, and Darwin noticed a horizontal seam of white calcareous rock running through a cliff some 45 feet above the sea. Upon closer inspection, he found that the white seam contained compressed seashells and coral. This seam had evidently once been the surface of the sea bed. Applying his recently acquired principles of geology, Darwin reasoned that a stream of lava must have flowed from the volcano, covering the sea bed. This must later have been heaved clear of the surface by volcanic pressure, to form the island cliff. But Darwin realized that this could not have taken place in a single cataclysmic event, as described by orthodox geologists. The seam of white rock had remained intact, as had the fragile seashells and coral embedded in it. The island must have been formed by a succession of volcanic events – each of which had pushed the seam a little further above the surface of the sea, allowing it to remain intact.

Darwin was already beginning to question orthodox geology (despite his rather brief acquaintance with the subject). Despite Henslow's warning, he found himself inclined to believe that Lyell was right. Other orthodoxies too began to come under question. As the *Beagle* sailed south of the equator, Darwin began lowering a net in the wake of the ship to catch plankton. Each day he found the net filled with all manner of miniature sea creatures 'most exquisite in their forms and rich colours'. At night in his cabin he pondered on the meaning of his findings. Why was there 'so much beauty' hidden away in the depths of the ocean where no one could see it? All this appeared to have been 'created for such little purpose'.

Darwin was beginning as he was to continue. Theory was all very well, but it was the vast accumulation of new facts on his voyage which stimulated him most. He wanted to collect *everything*: the facts and specimens piled up in an unceasing accumulation. Everything was grist for the mill: observed with keen delight, and then pondered upon. Why was it like this? How did it come to be like this? What was happening to it? Such were the questions nagging at the edge of his mind as the *Beagle* began its long journey down the east coast of South America. Darwin later described his mind as being in 'a perfect *hurricane* of delight and astonishment'.

This was all very well, but in his enthusiasm the ship's botanist had now passed beyond botany. 'Geology carries the day,' he declared in an enthusiastic letter home. The tyro-geologist had already decided to use the experiences gained aboard the *Beagle* to write a revolutionary new book about geology. He began taking copious notes (enough eventually to fill *three* books). Fortunately, his geology sorties ashore led him across terrain which also contained exotic local flora – thus providing a passing opportunity for the ship's botanist to fulfil his function.

In fact, Darwin remained an enthusiastic

botanist, despite his overriding new passion for geology. His intellectual eruption – for it was no less – had drastically altered his entire view of the scientific landscape. It would take him some while to focus and get his bearings in this unfamiliar territory, but there was no doubting its novelty. As he rushed ashore, collecting and delivering on board a regular cornucopia of plants, flowers, fossils, minerals and so forth, he gradually became aware of a somewhat deeper emptiness than that of the landscape he was denuding. And this emptiness seemed to lie at the heart of his new enthusiasm as well as his old one.

Geology and botany were making tremendous advances (single-handedly, it sometimes seemed) – yet both remained lacking in any central conceptual framework. Linnaeus may have drawn up a classification for different species, but how were they linked? What was the relation between the vast quantity of species scattered across the globe in such profusion? And what was the relationship between living species and those which occurred as fossils? Surely there had to be some scheme of things which brought them all together? In his initial enthusiasm Darwin was only dimly aware of such questions. Yet these were the ideas which were beginning to form at the back of his mind. All this abundance needed order: his life, his work, and the world around him – all required it, if they were not simply to disperse themselves in aimless fecundity. Captain FitzRoy, faced with an increasing jungle below decks, wasn't the only one who demanded to know: 'What *is* all this?'

In August 1832 Darwin embarked on a month-long expedition into the interior from Montevideo. On this, and subsequent expeditions into the Argentinian hinterland, he was to make some sensational finds. Fossilized bones from unknown animals of 'great dimensions' were discovered. He came across the petrified remains of a sloth as large as a rhinoceros, of giant armadillos, of dragon-like creatures with armour and club-like tails – all of which 'the revolutions of the globe seem to have destroyed'. There was now do doubting that Linnaeus's view of Creation was wrong. Species were not permanent. Animals which no longer existed had once roamed the earth. Yet curiously, there appeared to be a lack of similarly-aged fossils from species which *did* still exist. Could this mean that modern species had not existed at the same time as these disappeared species?

Such questions had been circulating for several years. But the traditionalists had long since found answers to them. The most convincing of these was proposed by the French biologist Georges Cuvier, who established himself as a kind of 'bishop of science' in late 18th century Paris. Miraculously riding the tide of the Revolution, the Empire and the Restoration, Cuvier also survived the gastronomic revolution which ensued when unemployed chefs to the aristocracy began opening the first gourmet restaurants in Paris. But this heroic survival had its price. Cuvier became so fat that he was nicknamed the 'Mammoth', and even went so far as to design a resplendent purple velvet robe bedecked with medallions to mask his figure on public occasions. Cuvier's scientific stature was of a similar enormity. He improved upon Linnaeus's classification, introducing new related species and classes, but still rejected the idea of evolution put forward by his contemporary compatriot Lamarck. According to Cuvier, nature was 'an immense network' of interlinked species, but it 'made no jumps'. In his view fossils, such as those later to be discovered by Darwin, were just further evidence for the Catastrophism, which saw the earth as formed by a series of cataclysmic upheavals, the most recent of which had been the Biblical Flood. Inevitably, such catastrophes had killed off life forms, and after each global catastrophe life had begun anew. This accounted for the disappearance of species which appeared in fossils, and the appearance of later species which were not found in fossilized form.

Darwin turned to his volume of Lyell, to see what his new mentor had to say. Lyell argued that the lack of modern species amongst ancient fossils of mammoths and the like was due to physical causes. They simply lacked durability. The shells and smaller bone structures of modern species were mostly not tough enough to survive the petrification process, and those which had undergone this process had simply been fragmented over time and ground away.

Darwin was left in a quandary. Cuvier's explanation was both ingenious and plausible, though he naturally couldn't help favouring

Lyell's approach. The latter's Gradualist conception seemed to be confirmed by what he had seen in the cliff at São Tiago, and by similar observations on the South American mainland. But when set against the factual evidence, both theories had their flaws. As Darwin began to collect more and more facts, his embryonic beliefs began to grow. Ultimately, his confidence would reside in his precious specimens – not the theories of others.

On one of his expeditions ashore Darwin made an exciting find which appeared to contradict both Lyell *and* Cuvier. Whilst exploring a cave he discovered the fossilized remains of some extinct giant armadillos. What was so remarkable about these giant fossils was that they were uncannily similar to the smaller armadillos which could still be found alive in the region. It looked very much as if these two species were somehow related. But how could they be, if they weren't even contemporaneous?

Late in 1832, when the *Beagle* put in at Buenos Aires, Darwin received the copy of volume II of Lyell's *Principles of Geology* which he had requested from London. To his surprise, Darwin found himself disappointed by the second half of Lyell's work. Despite Lyell's Gradualism in geology, he attacked Lamarck and was utterly opposed to any notion of evolution. In biology he remained an ardent Creationist – maintaining that each species had originated at the Creation.

During the long evenings at sea, Darwin would occasionally bring up such matters with Captain FitzRoy, who was undoubtedly one of the brightest young men in the navy. The Admiralty had entrusted FitzRoy with a vital mission, which required both expertise and initiative. Only fragmentary and often inaccurate Spanish charts existed of the South America coastline. A detailed survey of these seas would provide the British Navy with safe passage around Cape Horn and access to the Pacific. As if this dangerous and painstaking task wasn't enough, FitzRoy was also conducting his own researches into mapping the weather at sea. This was to establish him as one of the founders of the so-called science of meteorology. (By coincidence, Darwin's cousin Galton was to be the other leading light in this field.) As with many an energetic intellectual, FitzRoy also held firm

views on subjects which he knew nothing about.
He was a vociferous believer in Creationism, and
his views on landlubber society were similarly
primeval. FitzRoy was utterly opposed to the
long overdue Reform Act which had just passed
through parliament, giving the middle classes the
vote. FitzRoy also ran a tight ship. In line with
current naval practice, the men would be pub-
licly flogged whenever they crossed him on the
slightest matter. Darwin was expected to attend
these gruesome ceremonies, which plunged his
sensitive nature into a deep turmoil. When
Darwin happened to mention his anti-slavery
views at the captain's table, he received a verbal
flogging. Darwin was bluntly informed that he
talking cock and bull. Why, primitive people
were only fit for slavery 'as you'll find out when
we get to Patagonia.'

Darwin was indeed deeply astonished when he
encountered his first Patagonians. In grim
weather similar to an English winter, the ship's
cutter put ashore near the southern tip of Tierra
del Fuego, less than 100 miles from Cape Horn.
On the beach they were greeted by shrieking
naked savages flailing their arms and making

'hideous grimaces'. Some of the Patagonians weren't even frightened by rifles – simply because they had no idea how such things worked. The sound of gunfire was not associated with the stick-like object in a sailor's hand, and the ensuing bullet wound was regarded as some kind of mysterious spontaneous affliction. Despite his liberal views, Darwin found himself doubting that they were even 'fellow creatures'. Instead, he likened the Patagonians to 'the troubled spirits of another world'.

Darwin had begun the voyage an orthodox Christian, but his belief had faltered in the face of his scientific experiences. Similarly, his liberal belief in the essential equality and goodness of humanity suffered a serious blow when he encountered the vicious anarchic Patagonians living in their frigid wilderness. Darwin never lost his principles, but his reactions at the time were indicative. He was adrift, his mind free: open to almost any suggestion prompted by his new and varied experiences. Was it possible that these Patagonians were a species somewhere half-way between man and animals?

Darwin was essentially a timid character, who

avoided confrontation of any sort. He soon learned to keep his thoughts to himself at the captain's table. More surprisingly, he seems to have similarly repressed any such conflicts within his own character. His experiences, his new adventures in science, his encounter with Lyell's ideas on geology, and the same man's illogical rejection of evolution – all these must have produced a turmoil of contradictory reactions in Darwin. Yet there is little evidence that he confronted such contradictions.

In fact, the very opposite. Darwin appears to have suppressed them. Psychological opinion is generally agreed that Darwin's mind worked like that of an artist. These suppressed conflicts lay largely unexamined at the bottom of his mind – waiting until such time as they coalesced of their own accord, and could rise to the surface in this more acceptable form.

Such psychiatric sleight of hand may appear dubious, and explains nothing of the actual content of Darwin's ideas. Yet there's no denying that some similar process took place in Darwin's behaviour towards Captain FitzRoy. The fact is, they got on well together. For the most part, Darwin actually liked FitzRoy – all thought of his obnoxiousness simply banished from his mind. (Though this too would rise to the surface when he later wrote about his voyage.)

The self-effacing Darwin may have been no match for the brilliant aristocratic FitzRoy, but he seems to have been accepted by him, if only as a sort of enthusiastic boffin-mascot. The man who would produce one of humanity's greatest ideas was graciously patronized by the pioneer of meteorology.

Darwin's devotion to science evidently intrigued FitzRoy, and sometimes he would accompany Darwin on his expeditions ashore. Here Darwin would come into his own: scientific enthusiasm transforming the seasick wimp into a gung-ho adventurer whose stamina was equal to that of any man on board. (Though the sailors' lack of gusto for dashing up icy water-falls in the Andes, in search of weeds and bits of stone, may have sapped their stamina somewhat.)

There was something exceptionally powerful in Darwin – though he was the last to recognize this. His unassuming self stood aside from the powerful force which drove his mind. Even his mollycoddled hypochondria was simply forgotten when it came to his scientific pursuits. Yet he didn't really know what he was doing. Darwin hadn't even admitted to himself that he had found his vocation. In accordance with his father's wishes, he still accepted that he would enter the church at the end of the voyage.

But this remained thousands of miles and very many months away. Three years after setting out, Darwin was still collecting his specimens and the *Beagle* was still engaged in its survey. By early 1835 the *Beagle* had begun diligently mapping the chaotic myriad of inlets and islands which make up the south-western coast of South America. This was, and remains, the most intricate and treacherous stretch of coastline in the world: over a thousand miles of storm-tossed sea, with the mainland often separated from open water by over a dozen close-packed rocky islands. (In some stretches the charts made by the *Beagle* are still in use today.) As Darwin put it in a letter home: 'Everything in America is on such a grand scale . . . for such geology one requires six-league boots.'

But nothing could prepare him for the events of 20th February 1835, when Chile was struck by one of the worst earthquakes of the century. 'I was on shore and lying down in a wood to rest myself. It came on suddenly,' recalled Darwin. He tried to get up, but was reduced to his hands and knees. Vertigo swirled through his head as he grabbed at the ground, which rose before his very eyes. Fortunately, the Beagle was in a safe anchorage and remained undamaged. Ten days later, when they arrived off the city of Concepción, Darwin learned what their fate might have been. 'The whole coast was strewed over with timber and furniture as if a thousand great ships had been wrecked.' The survivors told him of what had followed the earthquake. In Darwin's words: 'a great wave was seen from the distance of three or four miles, approaching in the middle of the bay with a smooth outline . . . as it swept onwards with irresistible force . . . it broke in a fearful line of white breakers, which rushed up to a height of twenty-three vertical feet.' Cannons were swept inland like so much flotsam, an entire schooner was pitched 200 yards from the shore into the midst of the already ruined city. Ashore, Darwin gaped at a crumbled wall surrounded by petrified waves of rubble: all that was left of the great cathedral. But by now the novice geologist-botanist had developed a perceptive scientific eye: 'the most remarkable effect of this earthquake was the permanent elevation of the land [which] was upraised two or three feet.' He had now seen what previously he could only surmise.

Later that same year Darwin set off on a month-long expedition into the Andes. At over 10,000 feet he came across fossil shells. He began to understand 'the manner of force, which has elevated these great mountains'. Here, and in the earthquake, was irrefutable evidence backing Lyell's Gradualist theory of how the earth's crust had been formed. The earth's features had slowly emerged, forced up by huge volcanic pressures. Great land masses had formed. And perhaps other land masses had sunk, isolating continents? Could this perhaps account for such things as the existence of almost identical ostriches in Africa and South America, two continents which were totally separate?

Fortunately for the crew of the *Beagle*, who

were not enamoured of having their quarters transformed into a below-deck conservatory, arrangements were made to ship Darwin's multiplying collection of specimens back to Britain. Pressings from entire potted rainforests, together with wildernesses of fossils and labelled stones, were crated up and off-loaded onto returning merchantmen. Accompanying these were letters to Henslow, in which Darwin described his findings and began tentatively trying out his new ideas on his benefactor.

As the evidence mounted, Darwin's confidence gradually began to grow. Darwin was too timid to build his theories on anything but the broadest foundation of facts. But such were the quantity and quality of his findings that even Darwin was tempted to generalize. He was witnessing things on nothing less than a continental scale, prompting him to speculate about universal laws.

Back in Britain, Henslow was highly excited by the cornucopia of specimens arriving from his former pupil. He welcomed Darwin's findings and comments with enthusiasm, even going so far as to deliver a series of lectures on the subject at the Geological Society of London. These created quite a stir. In scientific circles, Darwin became something of a celebrity. Unaware of this, he continued making full use of his every moment before the dreaded day when he would have to give it all up and enter the church.

The high point and intellectual culmination of Darwin's voyage came with his visit to the Galápagos Islands. This isolated Pacific archipelago, consisting of 20 or so islands and various rocks, lies 600 miles east, off the coast of Ecuador. Three years prior to the arrival of the *Beagle*, the Galápagos Islands had been claimed by Ecuador and turned into a penal colony, run by an English governor. The only visitors were the occasional passing whaler. Darwin was to be there for just over a month: 15th September to 22nd October 1835. But what he saw there would one day change the world.

Darwin's first impressions were not inspiring. The islands were volcanic, with parched black volcanic rock. The equatorial climate was stifling, and the rank vegetation stank. Darwin likened the islands to 'cultivated parts of the Infernal regions'.

But the unusual animal and plant life that had grown up in this isolated world quickly took his interest. He observed giant tortoises, iguanas and a wide variety of finches. The giant land tortoises had mistakenly been called *galápagos* (turtles) by the original Spanish visitors, hence the islands' name. Darwin learned that these tortoises belonged to a species which had become extinct in other parts of the world. The iguanas here swam in the sea and fed off seaweed, quite unlike the landbound iguanas of central America – to which they were unmistakably related. Even more remarkable were the finches. Darwin found that these appeared in different sub-species on different islands. From island to island the finches had different colours, and a range of differing beaks. The beaks varied considerably in shape and size, in accordance with their different methods of feeding. On some islands the finches used their beaks to crack nuts, on others they had learned how to use cactus spines to probe in nooks and crannies for grubs, and yet others used their beaks to suck up nectar from flowers – and in each case their beak was appropriate for the purpose. As Darwin later recorded in his *Journal*:

'One might really fancy that from an original paucity of birds in this archipelago, one species had been taken and modified for different ends.'

It took the *Beagle* almost a year to return home, journeying on around the world by way of Australia, the Cape of Good Hope and Brazil. In all, the projected two-year trip had lasted almost five years. Darwin was now 27 years old. The raw botanist who had embarked upon the voyage disembarked a fully-fledged scientist possessed of an admirably rigorous technique (a mountain of facts to make a molehill of theory). And during the last lap of his voyage he had even achieved a modicum of maturity, attempting to come to terms with himself. He had almost accepted the fact that he might not enter the church.

Darwin arrived in London to find that he had become something of a celebrity. Henslow's lectures had whetted the appetite of the scientific community. Darwin's collections of specimens were lodged in various museums in London and Cambridge, to be analysed and catalogued by the experts. Darwin himself was appointed a fellow of the Geological Society, and almost im-mediately afterwards elevated to its ruling council. A year later he was elected to the Athenaeum, the most exclusive gentlemen's club in London, and the following year he was appointed a fellow of the Royal Society. Darwin had arrived in no uncertain fashion.

Yet despite his new-found renown, Darwin remained true to form. What now really interested him were the implications of his scientific findings, but he was far too diffident to make these public. In private he began writing a series of notebooks in which he developed his ideas about 'the species question'.

At the same time he continued to feed his relentless appetite for facts – reading widely, assiduously visiting zoos, farms, botanical gardens, as well as flower and animal markets, searching for further information concerning variations of species. In the course of his quest he interviewed naturalists, gardeners, breeders and even street traders of caged birds. The wealth of conflicting ideas and information which he had absorbed during his long trip around the world, and largely suppressed, now began rising to the surface, preoccupying him. He was unable to avoid the clash of ideas any longer, and his notebooks became a succession of questions and answers, statements and contesting queries. The long argument between himself and his material had begun – a process which was to be as thorough and relentless as the continuing process of fact-finding which accompanied it.

There was now no overlooking the dis-crepancies between his observations and orthodox Creationism, as outlined in the opening book of the Bible. According to the first book of Genesis: 'God created every living creature that moveth . . . every winged fowl . . . and every thing that creepeth on the face of the earth.' Each of these species had been specifically designed for the environment which it inhabited. This was known as the Argument from Design. Thus: fish had gills which enabled them to breathe under water, birds had wings, and creepy-crawlies were equipped with lots of wiggly things which enabled them to creep and crawl. Each species was immutably what it was, because it had been made that way in order to live the way it did. This not only answered all questions, but was the Holy Writ. To question it was to question God's wisdom.

But there always has to be someone who asks awkward questions – even if he makes sure he keeps them to himself. Darwin was now a respected member of the Victorian scientific community, and had no wish to be drummed out of the club for blasphemy. Fifty years before Robert Louis Stevenson wrote his classic story, Darwin was already rehearsing the life of Dr Jekyll and Mr Hyde. In public the respectable Dr Jekyll remained every inch the Victorian gentleman, meanwhile in secret Mr Hyde imbibed his heady potion of blasphemous ideas, tearing at the very foundations of all that was sacred.

According to the Argument from Design which followed on from Creationism, members of a species living under similar circumstances should always resemble one another. (This was the environment for which they had been designed.) But Darwin had noticed that birds in the Galapagos Islands, and those of the same species living in the Cape Verde Islands, were in reality different – despite the fact that both groups of islands were virtually identical (remote, volcanic, tropical etc). In fact, the species living in the Cape Verde Islands were much closer to those found on the African mainland, whose environment was completely different. Was it possible that the birds on the Cape Verde Islands and those on the African mainland had a common ancestor? (Such a thing was quite impossible, according to the notion of static species held by the Creationists.)

Similarly, the finches on the different Galápagos Islands were each distinctly different – whereas according to Creationist theory they should have been identical, as they all shared the same environment. On the other hand there was the ostrich. In the pleasant climate of the Argentine pampas, Darwin had observed giant ostriches. Yet south in inhospitable Patagonia the ostriches were of a smaller species. Both of these closely resembled the African ostrich. According to Creationist theory, all these different ostriches had simply been created as separate species. But couldn't these different species be the result of the same original species developing and adapting itself to different circumstances in geographical isolation?

Under the influence of his heady potion, Mr Hyde was becoming convinced that genesis as described in the Bible was bunk. Nature wasn't immutable at all. Geology, animals, plants – all changed. Creation hadn't happened all at once: nature was an unfolding process. The world was not static, it was in a process of 'becoming'. (The implications of this were truly mind-boggling. Did this mean that even humanity wasn't a permanent species? The uniqueness of human beings, the human soul, humanity's role as the jewel and purpose of creation – were all these Victorian articles of faith as nothing? For the time being, Mr Hyde chose to keep such things to himself. One step at a time.)

As Darwin's specimens and drawings were painstakingly processed, ever more astonishing facts began to emerge, confirming him in his suspicions. According to the cataloguers, the finches from the Galapagos weren't simply different varieties, as Darwin had thought: they belonged to different species. It looked as if there must originally have been a single species on the islands; but this had somehow been replaced by several species, each adapted in a different way to its surroundings. There were two possible explanations for this: the new species had been created in order to replace the single species lost by extinction (a Creationist version) – or the new better-adapted species were descended from a single ill-adapted predecessor which had become extinct. In his notebook Darwin described this latter process as 'descent with modification'.

But how did this work? What was the mechanism behind this process? Darwin had received no scientific training in any academic sense, and had so far shown no evidence of exceptional intelligence. (His scientific celebrity was due entirely to his being in the right place at the right time, and possessing an insatiable appetite for collecting specimens – hardly marks of brilliance.) Yet at the age of 28 it was as if he suddenly discovered his imagination. Here was the creative spirit of a poet harnessed to an utterly prosaic obsession with facts. The result was to be a scientist of genius. Darwin's thinking during the three years after he disembarked from the *Beagle* was to transform our knowledge for ever. (Arguably, the idea which Darwin came up with has had more effect on everyday human knowledge than any other in history.)

In the secrecy of his notebooks Darwin

continued his thoughts. Question followed by evidence, objection followed by evidence: the almost indiscernable undertow of argument moved on beneath the brimming flood of facts. Progress was gradual, but inexorable. Nowhere in Darwin's notebooks is there any 'Eureka!' moment when he 'saw it all'.

However, even Darwin couldn't avoid the occasional moment of excitement. One of these occurred in October 1838 when he read *An Essay on the Principle of Population* by Thomas Malthus. In his *Autobiography* Darwin suggests that he read this essay for entertainment. However, it fits in so well with his systematic reading that he was probably fibbing. (Judging from his *Autobiography*, Darwin's life appears somewhat short on entertaining activities at this point, even by Victorian standards – perhaps he thought that reading an improving essay on population would fill the gap.)

The clergyman and pioneer sociologist Robert Malthus subscribed to the Biblical view that 'the poor are always with us'. In his celebrated *Essay on the Principle of Population* he bolstered this realistic pessimism with some fanciful economic argument. Universal happiness was a vain pursuit, for the population would always increase faster than the means of production. In an early example of economic method, he even conjured up some 'statistics' to support this view. If the population growth remained unchecked, it would increase in a geometric progression (eg, 2,4,8,16 . . .) Whereas the means of subsistence would always increase in an arithmetic progression (eg, 2,4,6,8 . . .) The population expanded to the limit, where it was constrained by disease, famine, war, lightning etc. Darwin already had wide knowledge of the struggle for existence in the plant and animal kingdoms, but Malthus's words crystalized the fluid argument taking place in his mind. 'It at once struck me that under these circumstances favourable variations would tend to be preserved, and unfavourable ones to be destroyed. The result of this would be the formation of new species . . . I had at last got a theory by which to work.'

Darwin had understood a crucial point. The notion of 'the struggle for survival' had been current in scientific circles for quite some time (and had been accepted by everyone else since time immemorial). Species fought savagely against species in the perennial war to preserve itself. Reading Malthus, Darwin suddenly understood that the struggle went on *within* each species too (a point which had also been obvious since time immemorial, to the poor). But Darwin not only realized what happened, and how it happened – he also understood the consequences of this. Individuals within the species competed, and those with dominant traits survived (eg, the finches with beaks best adapted to feeding and fighting, those with the most frightening bright feathers etc). Such dominant traits were thus reinforced in the breeding of subsequent generations. This was the mechanism by which dominant traits were emphasized, and the weakening traits disappeared. Darwin crucially diverted attention from inter-species competition to intra-species competition.

As we have seen, the notion that things evolve organically had been in the air for some time. Charles Darwin's grandfather Erasmus had been a notable early proponent, and around the same time the French biologist Georges Louis Buffon had independently elaborated the idea. As keeper of the Jardin du Roi and a well-known polymath, Buffon was able to back up his ideas with some convincing scientific arguments. Animal species were not fixed, they had evolved variations. In the course of such evolution vestigial features could be seen (such as pigs' toes, for instance).

But it wasn't until the next generation that his compatriot Lamarck gave evolution a more solid basis. Lamarck was the first to draw a comprehensive diagrammatic picture, showing how nature began from single cell organisms and proceeded up the evolutionary ladder to the supreme species, man. Lamarck was also the first to put forward a convincing explanation of how this process actually took place. According to him, each species had an 'inner feeling' which inclined it to ascend the ladder of evolution, and this resulted in the spontaneous generation of higher features. Also, traits and skills which aided survival could be passed on to the next generation, by means of 'inheritance of acquired characteristics'.

Lamarck's brilliant ideas had just one flaw: they were wrong. And as far as Darwin was concerned, they also suffered from another serious defect: they were dangerous. Darwin had been introduced to the ideas of Lamarck in his early days at Edinburgh, by his mentor Grant as they had wandered the seashore collecting specimens. But Grant's revolutionary ideas in favour of evolution had over the years made him powerful enemies in the scientific community.

In December 1838 Grant was eventually hauled before the committee of the Geological Society and disgraced. As a junior member of the committee, Darwin watched in silence while his senior colleagues – Oxbridge professors and senior clergymen – savaged Lamarck and evolution. Darwin's discomfort can only be imagined. Having little other scientific qualification but his seat on the committee, Darwin felt himself ill-equipped to contradict such academic and theological bigwigs. And what could he have said? He didn't agree with Lamarckian evolution (he was developing his own ideas). Even so, Darwin hardly comes out of this incident well.

This was a late rearguard action by the Creationists, and none the less fierce for that. The Copernican revolution had brought the heavens within the realms of science, now evolution threatened to do the same for Nature and Life itself. The natural world was the last place where the spirit of God held supreme. It was His creation – the works of nature may have behaved in a scientific fashion, but their actual creation was not the realm of science. And anyone who contradicted this was committing blasphemy. This was a criminal offence, and liable to prosecution. (Britain was, and remains, a Christian country. Its laws are rooted in this religion, regardless of whether it clashes with scientific reality or the religious indifference of the majority of its citizens.) The choice for Darwin was stark: funk or martyrdom (albeit of the social kind). Upholding the tradition of Aristotle and Galileo, Darwin decided against subjecting his ideas to public examination by scientific ignoramuses.

Darwin's ideas were now reaching a crucial stage, coalescing around his central idea of evolution. His widespread and continuing researches led him to reject Lamarck's idea of it as a ladder. Instead, Darwin saw evolution as a tree, with diverging branches. New species were like new branches developing out of the main tree and its earlier branches. These then divided into further branches, and so on.

Darwin's concept of evolution as an intra-species struggle also neatly disposed of the most convincing of the opposition theories. Namely, the Argument from Design. This argument had a strong intellectual pedigree, having been refined through the ages by philosophers of such merit as Plato, Kant and Ibn Sina (Avicenna).

In 1802 a version of this argument had been introduced to science by the British theologian William Paley, who had previously achieved fame for managing to prove logically that Christ had risen from the dead. Paley's version of the Argument from Design used the example of a watch being found in the desert. The intricate perfection of its mechanical parts would certainly convince its finder of the existence of a skilled watchmaker. How much more perfect was the design of the human eye, with its precisely placed lens and retina forming an exact image, which was immediately and clearly transmitted by the optical nerve to precisely the right part of the brain. The human eye was perfectly adapted to

its surrounding and requirements: such perfection could only be the work of a Perfect
Designer.

Darwin's theory attacked this argument on its
own grounds. No organism – from the simplest
cell to the 'perfection' of human beings – was
perfectly adapted to its surroundings. If it was, it
would have no need to struggle. Instead, all of
life consisted of an unceasing struggle between
species and within species. Far from perfection, it
looked more as if the whole thing was a huge
botch. Darwin's argument may have been messy
and unpalatable, but it accounted for the way the
world was. The Argument from Design was
intellectually more elegant, but it didn't actually
explain anything. We have no way of telling
which argument is more 'true', when both fit the
facts. The only way we can judge between such
theories is by discovering how useful they are,
how fecund in producing new ideas. The
Argument from Design was a mere ornament,
whereas Darwin's ugly idea was to prove the
most fruitful theory science had yet produced.

Indeed, the idea soon began to produce ideas
for Darwin himself. Darwin's reading of Malthus

had brought to his awareness the social realities of the Industrial Age in Britain. Conditions in the 'dark satanic mills' of Lancashire, the sweat shops and infernal foundries of the Black Country, and all around him on the teeming streets of Dickensian London: the evidence was all there. Here was material just as compelling as the natural world of the Galapagos and the fossils of South America. This was how evolution worked at the most 'advanced' end of the scale. The wan cheeky urchin mocking the paterfamilias in his shiny bowler hat, the young clerk surreptitiously eyeing the drunken woman sprawled in the gutter, the strutting sergeant in his scarlet jerkin – all this was evolution too.

Darwin's notion of the struggle for survival within species led him to understand the medium and purpose of divergence within a species. The struggle within a species took place on the individual level. Those individuals with traits which were best adapted to the circumstances would survive to pass on these traits. Meanwhile detrimental traits would vanish, as the individuals who carried them failed to survive and pass them on. All was in transition: strengthening or diminishing. In this way, entirely new species evolved. This was both the purpose of individuality in a species, and the method by which it operated. Darwin had not discovered evolution – Lamarck and others had done that. Darwin had discovered *what it was* and *how it worked*. This process he described as 'natural selection'. Strictly speaking, it is the 'theory of evolution by natural selection' for which Darwin is remembered.

But Darwin's question and answer sessions with himself weren't entirely devoted to science. By 1838 he was becoming interested in natural selection of a more personal kind. He was now an eligible 29-year-old bachelor, with an adequate private income, of some professional renown. Working long hours at his desk, Darwin had reverted to his old hypochondriac ways. The tanned enthusiastic specimen-hunter returned from circumnavigating the globe had given way to the chair-bound scholar who made an engrossing hobby of his ailments.

Darwin soon became aware that he was suffering from the alarming epidemic which was sweeping middle-class Victorian England.

Namely, sexual frustration. There seemed to be no socially acceptable cure for this disease – apart from marriage, which according to his fellow members at the club only made it worse.

Darwin started to ponder the question of marriage with the same thoroughness he devoted to evolution and his health. Apart frosm the unmentionable (sex), what did he really need a woman *for*? Darwin began listing the pros and cons of marriage. For: 'Children . . . constant companion (& friend in old age) who will feel interested in one . . . object to be beloved and played with . . . better than a dog anyhow . . . charms of music and female chitchat . . . *but a terrible loss of time.*' Against: 'Freedom to go where one liked . . . choice of society and *little of it.* . . . conversation of clever men at clubs . . . not forced to visit relatives . . . expense and anxiety of children . . . perhaps quarrelling . . . LOSS OF TIME. . . . cannot read in evenings . . . less money for books etc . . . if many children forced to gain one's bread. . . . (but then it is very bad for one's health to work too much) . . . degradation into indolent, idle fool.'

Despite his seemingly overwhelming arguments against it, Darwin decided on marriage. He was keenly aware of the sacrifices he was making: this meant that he would never 'see the Continent – or go to America, or go up in a balloon'.

Darwin had better things to do than waste his time gallivanting around the salons in search of a fashionable wife. He astutely came to the conclusion that what he needed was someone who was 'an angel and had money'. His first cousin Emma Wedgwood fitted the bill, and they soon became engaged. The Darwins and the prosperous Wedgwoods were already close. The previous year, Emma's brother had married Darwin's sister. In recognition of this sacrifice of ballooning opportunities and trips to Paris, Emma's brother had been given a bond for £5000 and had his allowance increased by £400 a year. (In those days a working man was very pleased if he earned £1 a week.) So Darwin knew what he was getting.

Emma Wedgwood was a plain but presentable Victorian maiden, who had been well in-doctrinated in the hocus-pocus of Victorian family life. The man was in charge, and a woman's place was in the home: she accepted her second-class citizenship without question. As her marriageable years had begun to slip by, she had kept her eye on her shy serious cousin with the distinguished eyebrows and bushy sideburns. The two of them were the same age. Once Darwin had made his intentions clear, her affection quickly blossomed into a low-burning love that would last for a lifetime. For a man who couldn't abide conflict, Darwin had made an excellent choice. His relationship with Emma was to be deeply harmonious from the start – something which the Victorians often managed very well. Removing the sting of high passion and personal expectation from marriage had its benefits.

Emma understood precisely what she was getting in Darwin, and was quite happy about this. In the first flush of enamourment, Darwin couldn't help confiding to Emma that he had just one burning passion in life: his work. He even began explaining to her what it was all about. Emma was quite intelligent enough to understand what he was saying, but was sensible enough not to be particularly interested. It disappointed her that evolution left no place for God in Darwin's life, but she accepted this, with rare equanimity. She would offer a routine prayer for his soul when she attended church on Sundays, but otherwise left it at that. Her task was to give him support as he applied himself to his work, and humour him in his hypochondria. She was there to provide him with a trouble-free home, and trouble-free children. Natural selection may have led to such things becoming extinct nowadays, but its discoverer was to depend upon them utterly.

Charles Darwin and Emma Wedgwood were married in January 1839. Soon afterwards they moved into a house in Gower Street, on the edge of Bloomsbury. At last Darwin had a chance to rescue many of his specimens from storage. He tried to turn their new dwelling into a museum, while Emma did her best to turn it into a home. The newly-weds were happy in their homely museum; and despite his forebodings about married life, Darwin was able to continue life much as before. He worked long hours in his study, continued to take walks in the zoo, and also frequented the street markets, especially those for caged birds.

A few months after his marriage Darwin published the *Journal* of his voyage on the *Beagle*. This was ideal for the Victorian reading public. For a start, it contained adventures in exotic places. However, lest all this became *too* exotic its young author was diverted from any inappropriate thoughts or actions by his obsession with geology and botany (thus rendering the work fit for a female readership). And the whole thing was made reassuringly homely by those unmistakable *Diary of a Nobody* touches: '*28 December*. Waked in the morning with an eight-knot-per-hour wind, and soon became sick, and remained so during the whole day.' Darwin's *Journal* of his voyage was duly acclaimed as a classic travel book. This made its author into the contemporary equivalent of a popular TV scientist: jealous colleagues sneered, whilst the audience lapped him up (as long as he didn't start boring them with real science).

Darwin's popularity ensured that he was soon meeting similar celebrities of the day. He discussed the state of the nation with the earnest Scottish thinker and Germanophile Thomas

Carlyle; he listened with incomprehension to the progressive social homilies of the early feminist Harriet Martineau; and was enjoyably baffled by the company of Charles Babbage, the brilliant mathematician and eccentric inventor of the computer. He was also pleased to meet at last the geologist Charles Lyell, whose work had so inspired him during the long nights on the *Beagle*. Perhaps most importantly, he met Joseph Hooker, the great botanist who shared Darwin's obsession with specimens. Hooker travelled the five continents in search of rare botanical specimens, and ended up as director of Kew Gardens. Like Darwin, Hooker was no mindless collector, and their discussions on the theoretical implications of their findings confirmed Darwin in his convictions.

But London life did not suit Darwin. The 'pea-souper' fogs and sulphurous chimney smoke from coal-burning fires played havoc with his hypochondria. (The East End of London quite often went without sight of the sun for over a week.) Darwin was plagued by an increasingly sapping fatigue, which was accompanied by debilitating intestinal disorders and nausea. Part of this was certainly psychosomatic. In many ways, Darwin was close to being a psychological basket case. Never a robust character, he was dominated by his boorish father. Yet even if he wasn't fit, Darwin was undeniably a survivor. Despite not knowing what he wanted to do with his life, he had managed to evade his father's intentions for him. Incompetence and aversion had stopped him from becoming a doctor. And to put off entering the church, he had gone to sea. (Indicatively, having put half the world between himself and his father, Darwin flourished – becoming almost manically enthusiastic, proving himself as fit as the sailors, and having his first inklings of the ideas which were to make him world famous.) Darwin's scientific renown on his return had finally persuaded his father: it was unlikely that his atheist son would succeed in the church.

Darwin was aware of the grotesque social injustices of Victorian Britain, and as a consequence felt a deep guilt over his inherited wealth. But he knew that he needed this money to continue his work. (There were no Guggenheim fellowships in those days; and besides, his only

real qualification was a BA (divinity).) Throughout his life Darwin was to depend upon income
from his investments, and suffered nightmares
about being left penniless by a stock market
collapse. In modern parlance, Darwin spent a
great deal of effort avoiding 'facing up to
himself'. Fortunately for us, this effort diverted
his energies into obsessive work.

There's no denying Darwin's masterly hypochondria, which involved many hours stretched
out on the sofa receiving motherly attention
from Emma. However, later commentators have
shown that this may not have been all his own
work. Whilst hunting down specimens in the
Argentine, Darwin had been badly bitten by the
'black bug of the pampas' (*triatoma infestans*),
which is now known to be a carrier of Chagas'
Disease. The symptoms of this disease involve
persistent general lassitude, recurrent intestinal
disorders and other debilities which Darwin was
to exhibit for the rest of his days. But this should
not be allowed to eclipse the sheer stamina and
imaginativeness of Darwin's constant hypochondria – which he steadfastly maintained
throughout his long life. The figure stretched out

on the sofa, who enjoyed his wife Emma's loving attentions, had evolved from the child who luxuriated in the sentimental cosseting of his sisters. Darwin had never known the firmer practicalities of a genuine mother's love.

For the state of his health, Darwin moved out of London in 1842. Bankrolled by his father he bought a pleasant country house with a small estate in Kent for £2,000. Here, at Down House just outside Bromley, the 33-year-old Darwin settled down to the life of a semi-invalid. Yet he can't have been quite so infirm as he made out. Already Emma had given birth to the first two of their ten children.

By 1842 Darwin at last felt able to summarize his ideas on evolution by natural selection. A year or so later, he even wrote them out in more detail for Hooker – but still he decided against publication. Characteristically, he wished to avoid all controversy; and after Grant's fate at the hands of the scientific hierarchy he could well imagine how his ideas would be received. ('Creation not act of God', 'Victorian pater-familias claims descent from ape', etc.) But basically, the man who had produced the most daring idea in the history of science was simply not daring enough to reveal what it was.

This was to be no temporary aberration. As the years passed, and Darwin continued to sit on his secret, evolution became a subject of increasing scientific debate. In 1844 it even became a matter of public controversy, with the publication of an anonymous book called *Vestiges of the Natural History of Creation*. According to this work, fossil evidence showed that God's initial creation at the beginning of time had undeniably evolved. The suggestion that God's creation had been improved upon caused an outcry. There was widespread speculation about identity of the book's anonymous author. (Prostrate on his sofa, Darwin maintained a low profile at Down House.) According to one school of thought, the book was obviously written by a German. Someone even suggested it was the work of Queen Victoria's husband. (Sitting it out in Windsor Castle, Prince Albert too considered it best to maintain a low profile.) Finally it was discovered that the book had been written by a Scottish publisher called Robert Chambers. The royal household (and at least one lesser abode) breathed a sigh of relief, as Chambers was villified throughout the land.

Darwin had at last secured for himself the ideal conditions in which to work. He had also made a discovery of outstanding importance, on whose further implications he needed to elaborate. In the light of this, the project to which he now dedicated himself comes as something of a surprise. Darwin was to spend the next ten years of his life writing a treatise on the barnacle (*arthrobalanus*). Compared with evolution, the scope offered by this species was decidedly limited. Darwin himself described the male barnacle in the following manner: 'Mr Arthro-balanus [is] an enormous coiled penis.' Needless to say, Freudians have gone to town over Darwin's decade-long obsession with this unlikely organism. However, their ingenious and slanderous explanations are no less convincing than some others. One commentator has even claimed that Darwin's discussion about species of barnacles was in fact a thinly disguised version of his theory of evolution. He concluded that Darwin was 'using the barnacle as a stalking horse' (sic).

How long Darwin would have continued as the world's leading expert on a limpet resembling an enormous penis is difficult to ascertain. Fortunately our great scientist was awakened from his dogmatic slumbers by some sensational news. In the summer of 1858 he received a letter from Alfred Wallace, an ambitious naturalist of the upcoming generation.

Whilst an impecunious young teacher in Leicester, Wallace had read Darwin's *Journal* of his voyage on the *Beagle*. This had inspired him to dream of embarking on a six-year expedition to South America, to gather specimens of exotic insects and butterflies. After managing to persuade various museums and collectors to finance his expedition, he set off. Unfortunately, on the return voyage from South America his ship caught fire and almost all his specimens were lost. Employing what must have been considerable powers of persuasion, Wallace then managed to find new backers who financed an expedition to Malaya, which was to last 12 years. In 1858, four years into this expedition, Wallace was struck down by a bout of malaria in the Moluccas Islands in what is now eastern

Indonesia. (As these lie over a thousand miles from the Malay peninsula, he appears to have strayed a little from the persuasive itinerary presented to his backers.) Holed up in his hut, yellow-faced and trembling with fever, Wallace found his mind drifting through speculations about human evolution. He remembered how he had read Malthus's *Essay on Population*, and 'there suddenly flashed upon me the *idea* of survival of the fittest'. (The italics are important: these are later words recalling the event. As we shall see, the actual phrase 'survival of the fittest' has an interesting history of its own, and was not coined until six years later.) That night Wallace jotted down a summary of his theory by lamplight. It was this which Darwin received in the midst of his absorbing work on the barnacle.

'I never saw a more remarkable coincidence,' exclaimed the flabbergasted Darwin. In his letter, Wallace even used the same terminology that Darwin had used in his working notebooks over a dozen years previously!

Fortunately, Darwin's friends rallied round – most notably, Lyell, Hooker, and his new friend T. H. Huxley who gave popular lectures publicizing the latest scientific discoveries. These three friends arranged with the Linnaean Society for Wallace's theory and an abstract of Darwin's findings to be given as a joint paper on 1st July 1858. This succeeded in its contradictory aims. It papered over the cracks of any priority dispute, yet at the same time established that Darwin had got there first. Six thousand miles away on his remote jungle island, Wallace could do little but accept this *fait accompli* with good grace. (It would later become clear that Wallace's ideas in fact differed significantly from Darwin's – for instance, he believed that the higher mental capacity of humans could not be explained by natural selection alone, and required some kind of non-biological divine intervention.)

Darwin rapidly added the finishing touches to his two volume work *Living Cirripedia* (barnacles), followed by the two volumes of *Fossil Cirripedia*. Now at last he was free to start into a large-scale work setting down his ideas on evolution. This took him just a year to complete, and was published on 24th November 1859, under the title *On the Origin of Species by Means of Natural Selection, or the Preservation of Favoured*

Races in the Struggle for Life. Word had spread that Darwin was to produce a sensational new work, and the first edition of 1,250 copies sold out on the day of publication. New editions soon followed, and it was translated into languages from Bohemian to Hebrew, attracting controversy and commentary all over the world. As Darwin noted: 'an essay in Hebrew has appeared on it, showing that the theory is contained in the Old Testament!'

Others were less convinced of its religious pedigree. The backlash from the church was as inevitable as it was furious. Darwin's ideas left no room for divine intervention, and reduced human beings to the status of advanced apes. According to Darwin's argument human beings did not belong to a permanent divinely-ordained species, instead they were merely part of a continuously devoloping process.

T.H. Huxley engaged in an acrimonious public debate with the Bishop of Oxford, where Huxley was famously asked whether it was on his grandfather's or his grandmother's side that he was descended from an ape. The audience laughed, but Huxley won the day. His victory in this debate launched him on a new career publicizing Darwin's ideas.

These new ideas on evolution were also to have a major influence on Britain's major contemporary philosopher, Herbert Spencer, who became a leading exponent of what came to be known as 'social Darwinism'. It was Spencer who actually invented, and popularized, the phrase 'survival of the fittest'. But Spencer's social philosophy was based on a misunderstanding of Darwin. Ironically, Darwin's notion of evolution had been inspired by Malthus's picture of the struggle for survival in society. Darwin applied this to nature. Spencer then took Darwin's idea and reapplied it to society. Unfortunately, Spencer didn't use Darwin's idea as a means of interpreting the facts, but merely as a means to justify his own social ideas. Science deals with reality, while philosophy doesn't always feel itself limited to this mundane sphere. If the philosopher had left his study and spent more of his time in the slums he insisted upon philosophizing about, his philosophy might have born a Darwinian relation to the facts. As it was, Spencer's idea of evolution was more on a par with that of Darwin's grandfather Erasmus, and his philosophy on a par with Erasmus's epic poetry. It was T. H. Huxley who memorably described Spencer's philosophy as 'a deduction killed by a fact'.

Origin of Species launched the first big scientific idea in history to achieve popular fame. For the first time science claimed to 'explain everything', at least in the public mind. Darwin and evolution became the topic of the moment – much as Einstein and relativity were to become half a century later. But there was one major difference. Most people were convinced they *didn't* understand relativity. Alas, the opposite was the case with evolution. It was inevitable that Darwin's ideas should be hijacked and misinterpreted – by everyone from Spencer to the Bishop of Oxford. But Darwin's theory also faced some serious objections, which he realized had to be answered. If he insisted that evolution consisted of gradual change, how did he account for the fact that fossil findings often indicated the opposite? In many cases evolution appeared to jump over large gaps, with no intermediate species appearing. Darwin could only answer that one day these gaps would be filled by the discovery of intermediate fossils. (In fact he wasn't entirely right here. Modern archaeological evidence suggests that some life forms remain stable for lengthy periods, and are then succeeded with comparative rapidity by new forms.)

But there were further problems. The objections put forward by the Catholic zoologist St George Mivart were both precise and challenging. Fully developed organs (such as the eye) were of obvious evolutionary benefit. But what benefit were such organs in the early stages of their development? They must have begun as mere 'fortuitous novelties'. In its initial stages of development the incipient organ would have produced no advantage in the struggle for survival. According to Mivart, it was evident that such organs as the eye had developed in a purposive fashion – from random trait towards the function they would eventually fulfil.

Darwin challenged this idea head on. He maintained that an organ in its initial stage of development could be of advantage, just as much as an organ in its later stage. Though this advantage frequently served a different purpose. For example, the feather in its initial stage of development must have served to keep its owner warm; only later did it evolve to give aerodynamic advantage. Whereas the eye could well have originated from a light-sensitive spot on the surface of the skin, gradually evolving advantageous complexities such as the retina, the pupil and the optic nerve.

The fact is, of course, Darwin was right. In his words, it was a 'failure of imagination' not to see how things had evolved over the aeons in this fashion. It was necessary to look from the beginning forwards, not from the present backwards. To believe that the first primitive feather appeared in nature so that one day it could be used to fly was sheer mysticism.

Mivart's seemingly strong argument dissolved. But what of his religious beliefs? Mivart was in many ways a sympathetic figure, emblematic of the conflicts of his age. A devout believer in God, he was soon converted to Darwinian theory. But he also sought to reconcile his religion with his science. As a result, he was ridiculed by the Darwinians and excommunicated by the Catholic Church. Very much a man of his age, he was treated as such – by both those who lived in the past, and those who looked to the future.

For primitive warming bum-fluff to evolve into the magnificence of the albatross's wing, or the absurdity of the peacock's tail, evidently required time. And a great deal of it, according to Darwin's theory. The trouble was, all this evolution needed a lot longer than the time since the Earth had begun.

The Earth's age was still a matter of some dispute. In the 17th century, Archbishop James Ussher had calculated from biblical sources that the Creation had taken place in 4004 BC. This date was later improved upon by the great biblical scholar John Lightfoot, vice-chancellor of Cambridge University in Newton's time. According to Lightfoot's more exacting calculations, the creation had taken place at precisely nine o'clock in the morning on 23rd October 4004 BC. (This may appear laughable, but modern science is capable of almost equal absurdities on this topic. Though unable to calculate the universe's creation to within a billion years, contemporary scientists confidently describe what happened within a trillion trillionth of a second of the event.)

By Darwin's time progressive geologists such as Lyell had begun to accept that the Earth was hundreds of millions of years old. But it soon became clear that Darwin's evolution required an even longer period, possibly over a billion years. Not without a little grumbling, Lyell and the more advanced geologists of the period gradually accepted Darwin's somewhat elastic estimate. This cosy state of affairs was rudely disturbed by the pioneering Scottish physicist William Thomson, later to become Baron Kelvin. The son of a farm labourer, Thomson laid the first transatlantic cable and was possibly the first scientist to make a vast fortune out of his science. (His Glasgow mansion was the first house to be illuminated by electricity, and he invented a wide range of navigational instruments for his yacht.) But Thomson had a bee in his bonnet about 'geologists who uncompromisingly oppose all paroxysmal hypotheses' ie, his own Catastrophist theories about the earth's geological development. Basing his calculations on the temperature of the earth's interior, Thomson worked out that the world had begun to solidify not more than 400 million years ago, and possibly even as little as 20 million years ago. His figures were based on incontrovertible physics. There just wasn't time for Darwin's evolution to have taken place.

When Darwin's protagonist Huxley heard this news he was aghast. It looked as if his career as the leading Darwinist on the lecture circuit was ruined. Manfully he tried his best to squeeze the quart of evolution into the pint pot of the earth's age according to physics, but to no avail. Thomson's news also made Darwin sit up on his sofa. Faced with the prospect that his life's work had been sabotaged, Darwin departed at once for one of his regular health cures at the spas. Assiduously taking the waters, Britain's best-known atheist secretly prayed that Thomson had got his sums wrong.

As if by a miracle, Darwin's prayers were answered. (Though without causing the un- grateful beneficiary to modify his views on the divine.) It turned out that Thomson's figure was based on a faulty assumption about global cooling. Subsequent calculations were to increase the age of the Earth far beyond Darwin's requirements, to the point where it now stands at around five billion years. (The problem now is how to stretch out evolution: could it even have had periods when it just stopped for a bit?)

Such incidents serve to illustrate a serious point: one which is difficult for us to appreciate. Darwin's idea of evolution survived because it appeared too good an idea to be false. It explained so much of the complexity of the world – bringing vast areas within the scope of our understanding. Previously, we hadn't questioned why things were the way they were in any overall scientific way. Darwin's idea not only explained this, but showed how it happened – from barnacles to barons. Yet ironically, at the time Darwin's idea often owed its survival more to faith than to science. The evidence supporting it was far from conclusive. If Thomson's figures had proved irrefutable, as they appeared at the time, this would have meant the end of evolution. Darwin and Huxley clung on by faith, in the teeth of the evidence.

And worse was to come. After the success of *Origin of Species*, Darwin set about elaborating his idea in a further series of books. But by now he was faced with a further serious problem. This had been posed by the polymath Scottish engineer Fleeming Jenkin, a colleague of Thomson's in the cable-laying business. Jenkin pointed out that if natural selection worked as Darwin proposed, the individual with the dominant traits would inevitably dilute these traits when it interbred with the less endowed members of the species. This argument appeared irrefutable to Darwin. If genetic factors were divisible, dilution of dominant traits was inevitable.

Darwin decided that the only way to overcome this objection was to take the drastic step of abandoning natural selection. From the sublime to the ridiculous. In its place he proposed a theory first concocted in the fifth century BC by the Ancient Greek philosopher Democritus. This was known as pangenesis. The modernized version of this theory stated that each organ and substance of the body secreted its own characteristic particles, which then combined to form the reproductive cells. The particles secreted by each organ faithfully echoed not only the characteristics but also the comparative strength, size and health of the organ. This may have seemed all very well with regard to myopic green eyes or resilient long noses, but its further implications were less plausible. It meant that if an individual expanded his or her musculature by pumping iron, this physical grotesquerie would be passed on to the offspring. In other words, pangenesis led to Lamarckism, with its 'inherited characteristics'.

This time Darwin was wrong: he had in fact been right in the first instance, though he had no way of knowing this. The way hereditary characteristics are passed on had already been discovered by the Czech monk Gregor Mendel, working in isolation in a monastery at Bruno. Mendel had carried out exhaustive experiments over several years, tracing how the genetic factors exhibited by pea plants were passed on from one generation to the next. He had discovered that genetic factors didn't blend or become diluted – they were in fact *indivisible*. Thus Darwin's dominant traits would have been preserved, and not diluted as Jenkin suggested.

Unfortunately Mendel's findings had only been published in the magazine of the local Bruno

Biology Society, which didn't exactly boast a worldwide readership. As a result, Mendel's work remained unnoticed until the early 20th century – when Mendel was posthumously recognized as the father of genetics.

In order to save his theory, Darwin had been forced to jettison a central idea and take on board sheer fantasy. Yet despite reverting to outmoded Lamarckism, Darwin's notion of evolution somehow survived. A crude version of 'survival of the fittest' replaced the subtleties of natural selection.

In 1871 Darwin published *The Descent of Man*. This expanded his idea far beyond its initial physical manifestation. According to Darwin, evolution included both moral and spiritual traits. 'The highest possible stage in moral culture is when we recognize that we ought to control our thoughts.' Yet he emphasized that the time would soon come when 'it will be thought wonderful that naturalists, who were well acquainted with the comparative structure and development of man and other animals, should have believed that each was the work of a separate act of creation'. This led him to his celebrated conclusion: 'Man with all his noble qualities, with sympathy that feels for the most debased, with benevolence which extends not only to other men but to the humblest living creature, with his god-like intellect which has penetrated into the movements and constitution of the solar system – with all these exalted powers – still bears in his bodily frame the indelible stamp of his lowly origin.'

His ideas on sexual selection also bear the stamp of this lowly origin. Darwin noted that in the majority of species both the male and female young resemble the female. This led him to conclude that males were a more advanced state of evolution than females. His work in this sphere seems to been marred by an untypical lack of research, as well as conclusions drawn from the observation of just one specimen. Namely, his wife. Darwin concluded: 'The female is less eager than the male.' And she selects 'not the male which is most attractive to her, but the one which is least distasteful'. Despite strong scientific (and Victorian) opposition, Darwin insisted that in many species 'female choice' operated in the selection of sexual partners. Hence the peacock's tail, and the peahen's more restrained plumage.

On this score Darwin was firmly opposed by his unlucky co-discoverer Wallace, who remained content to play second fiddle to Darwin. Wallace had finally returned to Britain in 1864, after a decade of wandering through the Malay Archipelago at his backers' expense. He then embarked upon a career lecturing on what he was gracious enough to call 'Darwinism' (Wallace is even credited with coining this term). He made several further contributions to the subject. Not least was his criticism of Darwin's 'female choice' in sexual selection – for example in the peacock. Wallace argued that the need for camouflage and self-protection whilst nesting far better accounted for the relative dullness of female plumage. However, heartened by the success of his arguments he later overstretched himself. His attempts to introduce spiritualism, and then phrenology, into Darwinism were not greeted with enthusiasm by his erstwhile co-discoverer. Darwin wrote to him anxiously: 'I hope you have not murdered too completely your own and my child.'

Darwin continued to elaborate upon his

theory for the rest of his life. In 1872, at the age of 63, he published *Origin, The Expression of the Emotions in Man and the Animals*, which demolished any biological distinction between human beings and animals. Extensive research into the facial expressions and sounds emitted by animals showed that they too were capable of complex feelings such as anxiety, despair and selfless devotion – all previously considered to be uniquely human. This work as good as founded ethology, neurobiology and the study of psychological communication.

However, the man who could devote a decade to writing about the barnacle still had an ace up his sleeve. During his last years Darwin also produced a major work on another field of similar importance: *The Formation of Vegetable Mould, Through the Action of Worms, With Observations on their Habits*. This alas was to be his final masterwork. After enduring years of increasing invalidism (and unremitting study), Darwin died at the age of 73 on 19th April 1882. Though he had been given no state honours during his lifetime, he was to receive the ultimate accolade of being buried at Westminster Abbey.

A FEW FACTS & FIZZLES

• 'Survival of the fittest' is a tautology. All it really means is 'survival of what survives'.

There is no other criterion of 'fitness to survive'. What could there be? Usefulness? Stamina? Fierceness? Nature abounds in useless ephemeral beauty. The sheer lack of any criterion accounts for its cornucopia of unending variety.

Even Darwin contradicted himself on this point:

> 'I have called this principle, by which each slight variation, if useful, is preserved, by the term of Natural Selection'

And:

> 'What a book a devil's chaplain might write on the clumsy, wasteful, blundering, low, and horridly cruel works of nature'

• For many, including its founder, Darwinism was concomitant with atheism. It has contributed to the spread of godlessness in the 20th century, especially amongst scientists. Or has it?

In 1916 a poll of US scientists showed that 60% didn't believe in God. In 1997 a similar poll carried out amongst British scientists found that 40% did believe in God.

'Evolution is essentially a whimsical process, generously allowing for the survival of creationists, astrologists and even meteorologists'

John Mandeville

'Believing as I do that man in the distant future will be a far more perfect creature than he now is, it is an intolerable thought that he and all other sentient beings are doomed to complete annihilation after such long-continued slow progress. To those who fully admit the immortality of the human soul, the destruction of our world will not appear so dreadful'

Charles Darwin

'It may be doubted whether there are many other animals which have played so important a part in the history of the world, as these lowly organized creatures'

Charles Darwin, *The Formation of Vegetable Mould, Through the Action of Worms*

CHRONOLOGY OF DARWIN'S LIFE

1809 Charles Darwin born on 12th
February in Shrewsbury

1817 His mother Susannah Wedgwood dies

1818 Sent to Shrewsbury Public School

1825 Begins studies at Edinburgh
University Medical School

1828 Begins degree at Christ's College,
Cambridge, with a view to entering
the church

1831 On completion of his degree sets sail
for South America on the *Beagle*

1835 From September to October *Beagle* at
Galapagos Islands

1836 *Beagle* returns to Britain after
circumnavigation of the globe

1837 Starts Species Notebooks

1839 Marriage to his cousin Emma
Wedgwood. Publishes *Journal* of

voyage on the *Beagle*

1842   Moves to Down House in Kent.
        Makes first definitive summary of his
        Theory of Evolution by Natural
        Selection

1846–58 Working on barnacles

1858   Receives Wallace's shock letter on
        evolution from the East Indies

1859   Publishes *Origin of Species*, which
        immediately becomes bestseller and
        centre of raging controversy

1871   Publishes *Descent of Man*, further
        elaborating his theory

1881   Publishes *The Formation of Vegetable
        Mould, Through the Action of Worms*,
        his final work

1882   Dies at Down House 19th April.
        Buried at Westminster Abbey a week
        later

SUGGESTIONS FOR FURTHER READING

Charles Darwin: *Journal of Darwin's Voyage on the Beagle* (Cambridge, 1988 et seq.)

Charles Darwin: *Autobiography* (Collins, 1958 et seq.) Both the above are readable, interesting and often exciting – despite the personality of their author. Many popular edited editions include both works.

Charles Darwin: *Origin of Species* (Penguin, 1985 et seq.)

Charles Darwin: *The Descent of Man* (Princeton, 1981 et seq.) Evolution in detail from the horse's mouth: the above are his two masterpieces, and are for the most part easily comprehensible to the non-scientific reader.

Adrian Desmond and James Moore: *Darwin* (Michael Joseph, 1991) – An exhaustive biography – probably the best of the many.

David Kohn (ed): *The Darwinian Heritage* – A vast collection of essays by a variety of experts covering the whole Darwinian spectrum.